Environmental Toxins

Six Threats to the Natural World

Katie Yendis and Louis Bevoc

Published by
NutriNiche System LLC

Louis Bevoc books...simple explanations of complex subjects

Water pollution

Air pollution

Summary 42

Authors' perspective 42

Urban sprawl 44

Background 44

Effects 45

Solutions 47

Authors' perspective 50

Bonus Section - Green Business 52

Introduction 53

Triple-bottom-line 53

Sustainability 54

Common strategies 57

Soil Pollution

Background

Every human interacts with soil in some way, shape, or form. A potato farmer might have much more interaction than the captain of a commercial fishing vessel, but that captain has to walk on soil at some point. The point being made here is that soil is common ground (no pun intended) for everyone in the world. Based on this fact, soil pollution was chosen as the first environmental issue discussed in this book.

Soil pollution is almost always a result of human activities rather than natural occurrences, and it typically intensifies as industrial activity increases. It occurs when land comes into contact with biological, chemical, or physical contaminants. These contaminants will be discussed in the next section of this book, but first, the concept of soil pollution and the threat it presents to people and the environment need to be understood.

Soil contamination is a big concern of environmentalists due to the health risks involved and the time and money required to restore the earth to its original composition. Health risks result when people have direct contact with polluted soil, but they can also come from breathing the vapors that are omitted or drinking water that is found near or beneath the contaminated ground. Restoration of soil to its natural state requires people who are knowledgeable in chemistry, geology, hydrology, physics, and the environmental sciences. The high cost of restoration is a major reason why much of the land in the United States must pass certain types of environmental testing before it can be sold. Unfortunately, soil pollution is a big concern that needs to be addressed with somewhat drastic measures.

Aside from the health and environmental risks, soil pollution can also be very unsightly. Industrial waste, for example, makes landscapes appear as if they have gone through some type of nuclear mishap. This type of contamination is very obvious and can be seen with the naked eye from long distances. In fact, some areas of land polluted with industrial waste are so unappealing that people will not even let their dogs roam on or around it.

Another example of unsightly land is an oil spill that turns soil into a darkened hardened mass with an iridescent sheen that can appear green or purple depending on the angle or light exposure. This might seem like it would be attractive, similar to the Northern Lights seen in Alaska, but it pales in comparison. Instead, it comes across as dirty earth, similar to a neglected alley in a rundown neighborhood.

Regardless of the reason for soil pollution, it has a negative impact on humans and the ecosystem. This impact starts at very low levels. In fact, soil is considered polluted once levels of naturally occurring contaminants exceed normal levels. These contaminants include inorganic salts and metals, in addition to organic compounds such as lipids and proteins. They are formed by various types of natural activities including the decomposition of living matter absorbed from air or water. Soil found to be slightly contaminated might not pose a serious threat to people or the environment, but a contamination cutoff needed to be set at some point...so exceedance of natural levels was selected.

Effects

Soil pollution can be natural, but this book focuses on the pollution that is man-made. Its effects are considered serious because they pose risks for people and the environment, and they usually occur due to neglect, lack of concern, or limited choices.

The major effects are listed in terms of contaminants and described below.

Agricultural contaminants

These contaminants typically come from farm crops or livestock. Animal excrement, better known as manure, is a big contributor to agricultural pollution. If excrement is left untouched and uncleaned, it creates very unsanitary conditions that lead to the soil becoming toxic and pathogenic. Sickness can result from disease-causing organisms such as E. coli. The biggest concern about excrement contamination is that it does not stop until the animals producing it die.

Another form of agricultural contamination comes from pesticides. The public's demand for organic fruits and vegetables is in high gear, but that demand has not stopped farmers from using traditional chemicals to ward off pests. When chemical fertilizers fall or run off plants and trees, they embed themselves in the ground and poison the soil.

The last type of agricultural contamination occurs from herbicides. These chemicals destroy existing vegetation so new crops can be planted. Herbicides do a good job destroying just about everything, but they also pollute the soil beneath them…and the damage can be quite severe if large amounts of these chemicals are used.

Biological contaminants

Biological contaminants in the soil include bacteria, viruses, funguses, and parasites. An example of a disease-causing (pathogenic) bacteria is Clostridium, an example of a disease-causing virus is Hantavirus which occurs when rodent excrement contaminates the soil, an example of a pathogenic fungus is Blastomycosis which is transmitted from the soil via inhalation, and an example of a disease-causing parasite is Helminth which survives and thrives in soil during certain climate conditions. These biological contaminants might not be known by the average person, but they can present health problems for humans who are in or around soil…which includes just about everyone.

Chemical contaminants

Some of the chemical contamination of soil comes from agricultural operations in the form of pesticides and herbicides. However, there are other chemicals that infiltrate soil and cause potentially dangerous situations for humans and the environment. Gas oil spills are two common examples.

People usually associate these gas and oil spills with water pollution, but they also occur on land. In the past, these types of spills were purposeful so companies and individuals could get rid of unwanted gas and oil, but laws are now in effect that highly regulate this type of contamination. Today, most of these spills are accidental, and they can cause a lot of damage if they are not brought under control in a relatively short period of time.

Another type of chemical soil contamination comes from lead. In the past, lead-based paint was used to paint everything. It was banned in the late 1970s for health reasons, but the lead from paint used decades ago still contaminates soil today. In some cases, new topsoil has to be placed over the old soil before planting so the roots do not reach the lead in the ground below. This is a very expensive process and it is not guaranteed to work, so it is understandable why lead from any source is a major concern of environmentalists.

Consumer and commercial contaminants

Not surprisingly, the biggest threat to soil contamination comes from humans. Their daily activities introduce impurities into the earth that immediately or eventually cause damage. This makes sense because, after all, soil functions as the "world's kidney" by filtering out contaminants before they are absorbed internally. This means soil receives the brunt of the harmful contaminants, and those contaminants are transferred to humans through absorption, inhalation, or ingestion. Absorption occurs when people touch the soil, such as a child playing outside. Inhalation occurs when people breathe in air-borne particles from the soil, such as a construction worker who moves soil while building a foundation for a building. Ingestion is more second-hand because it comes from edible plants that grow in the soil and pick up its contaminants.

Typically, greater amounts of human activity increase the chances of contaminating the soil. This activity can come from something simple, such as walking down a path made by others, or something complex, such as the building of an athletic stadium. In short, if soil is disrupted and has its composition altered with foreign additives or too much of something that naturally exists, then it is considered contaminated. The negative effects of this contamination are wide-ranging and the environment pays the price.

Solutions

People's awareness of soil pollution has inspired world-wide thinking about reducing or eliminating its negative effects. The complete "cleaning" of soil is not practical or possible, but the toxicity can be reduced via a few different corrective actions. There are also ways to prevent the contamination from taking place; thereby negating the need for those actions. Below are some examples of corrective actions and preventative measures that are currently being used to combat soil pollution.

Corrective actions

As noted above, corrective actions help to rid the soil of contaminants and restore it to its natural balance. None of the methods below work perfectly, but they are all beneficial in some way. At the very least, they stop the environmental harm from getting worse, and at the very best they reverse the process and restore the soil to its natural form.

One type of corrective action involves adjusting pH. Essentially, pH refers to the alkalinity or acidity of soil, and it can affect the strength of pollutants. Neutral soil (pH = 7) works best for reducing the negative impact of contaminants. This means soil that is acidic (lower than pH = 7) or alkaline (greater than pH=7) allows pollutants to prosper. Natural compounds, such as limestone or calcium carbonate, can be added to adjust the pH.

Another type of corrective action is known as chemical fixation. Chemical fixation works on chemical pollutants in the soil using a chemical reaction. Essentially, it mixes the contaminated soil with "clean" soil and chemical additives; thereby producing material that prevents leaching by binding contaminants.

The third type of corrective action involves the addition of healthy organic material to the contaminated soil. Composted greenery and aged animal manure can be used to build a "shield" that protects plants growing within.

The final type of corrective action is known as bioremediation. In this process, microorganisms designed to break down contaminants are added to the soil. This procedure is the most environmentally friendly and natural because the microbes allow the soil to restore itself back to its original composition.

Preventative measures

As noted above, preventative measures prevent contamination from occurring; thereby eliminating the need for corrective actions. If properly implemented and monitored, these measures work toward keeping soil clean by maintaining its natural balance.

Controlled farming is the first type of preventative measure. This measure reduces soil erosion by preventing overgrazing of land by livestock and overplanting of crops by farmers. Soil remains rich and fertile and poses no threat to humans or animals.

The second type of preventative measure is reforestation...which is the opposite of deforestation. This measure involves people replacing every cut tree with one or two planted trees. It prevents soil erosion from occurring while providing resources for the future; thereby creating a win-win situation.

Recycling is the third type of preventative measure. This measure has rapidly increased in popularity over the past few decades because the public is becoming increasingly concerned about the environment, especially when it comes to pollution and waste. Waste that used to be put in the ground is now being made into new products; thereby preventing the contamination that could have occurred. Biodegradable material, an extension of recycling, has also become fashionable because it is easily broken down in soil; thereby preventing the contamination that used to occur from materials that took 25 years or more to break down.

The last and possibly most obvious preventative measure is the reduction of herbicides, fertilizers, and pesticides. These contaminants often pose the biggest threat to soil pollution, and reducing their usage will greatly impact the quality and safety of the ground where they are used. Similar to reforestation, this measure also creates a win-win situation because plants have more natural nutrients for growth and disease is not passed on to humans.

Summary

Soil pollution is unsightly and has the potential of spreading disease to people thought absorption, inhalation, or ingestion. It usually occurs from human activity in the form of agricultural, chemical, biological, consumer, or commercial contamination. It is somewhat difficult to correct once it has occurred, but it can be prevented by adjusting the behavior of people and organizations.   In short, soil pollution is a problem today that can be ended with the effective use of preventative measures.

Authors' Perspective

In terms of destruction, we believe soil pollution is one of the most challenging types of pollution in the world...with little or no hope of ever being controlled. It destroys huge areas of land and can take decades, even centuries, to reverse the impact it has on the world. It spreads disease, kills wildlife, and creates ugly landscapes in urban, suburban, and rural environments. It is like a tornado that disassembles the environment and throws the pieces anywhere and everywhere.

However, the devastating effects of soil pollution are not the reason that we have lost hope for a resolution to this problem. We believe the problem is due to an economic divide. In short, it is a direct result of the division between people who have money and those who do not. People with money have their essential needs taken care of; thereby allowing them the freedom to view soil pollution as a problem that can be fixed with preventative measures. They do not live off the earth, so they can join the fight to preserve it.

Unfortunately, many poor people need to survive off the earth. They do not have the option of controlled farming because their cattle need to graze due to a lack of money to purchase other types of food. These animals' contributions to agricultural contamination cannot be controlled because there are no programs available for the elimination of their waste. Along the same lines, poor farmers cannot avoid overplanting because they must grow crops in the limited space they have available to survive. They are not paid by their governments to "not plant" so the soil on the farm becomes eroded.

Poor people are also financially unable to implement reforestation programs because they do not have the money necessary to purchase the replacement trees. If their governments do not support the reforestation cause, then the harvested areas are left baron and soil erosion takes effect.

Recycling is a great idea...for people who can afford to do it. Poorer communities do not have the resources to recycle and, as a result, the soil becomes contaminated. Biodegradable materials are expensive, and that expense is deemed unnecessary when people are struggling to feed their families.

The reduction of herbicides, pesticides, and fertilizers is possible for poor people, but only if it is the least expensive option. For example, some farmers cannot afford any type of pesticides, so, by default, they grow "organic" crops. However, those who can buy pesticides are not going to spend more money simply for soil pollution prevention. Their goal is to preserve their crops to obtain the greatest yield possible. If less expensive but more destructive pesticides do the job, then they are going to be used.

In summary, soil pollution is not a concern for those who live day-to-day, are unable to save, and have no idea of what the future holds. They are much more concerned with their own longevity rather than the longevity of the ground beneath them.

Acid Rain

Background

The term "acid rain" is scary to many people. They think of it as a burning rain that could melt away their skin upon contact, similar to the effects of being sprayed with concentrated hydrochloric acid. Fortunately, acid rain does not harm humans. It has many detrimental effects, as will be discussed later in this section, but human health is not negatively impacted.

Acid rain is made up of water (rain, sleet, fog, snow, etc.) and acidic contaminants (gases or particles). It has an acidic pH, typically lower than 5.7, due to elevated levels of hydrogen ions. This book is not designed to go into discussions on chemistry, but it is important to understand that acid rain almost always results from chemical actions stemming from pollution. As might be expected, this pollution comes from human actions rather than the natural environment.

Effects

As noted above, acid rain is not harmful to humans. They can walk in it and even bathe in it without health concerns. However, the sulfur and nitrogen gases and particles that contaminate the rain are harmful when humans are exposed to them. They can cause respiratory diseases in some people and worsen the respiratory issues that others are already experiencing such as asthma or bronchitis.

Acid rain might not pose threats to humans, but it does do other damage. Sometimes this damage is barely noticeable because it takes place over long periods, but other times the impact is immediate. Below are some examples of the damage that can occur.

Water

This refers to the water in lakes, rivers, streams, ponds, and wetlands. Acid rain, especially during heavy downpours, lowers the pH of these waters below the normal 6.5 which creates problems for the animals that live within. This is partially due to heavy metals becoming soluble in acidic environments. Copper, aluminum, and lead are released into the water instead of being absorbed in the sediment at the bottom. As the concentration of these metals increases, the water becomes toxic to fish and animal life. Species threatened include frogs, crayfish, trout, and bass. However, even worse, the resulting imbalance of nature puts the entire ecosystem at risk. Based on the damage potential, it is relatively easy to see why people are concerned about acid rain contaminating water.

Oceans are also impacted by acid rain, but the effect is mostly limited to coastal ocean water that is closest to the pollution on land. Motorized vehicles, manufacturing plants, and farms all pollute the atmosphere causing rain on the coasts to become acidic. That rain lowers the pH of the coastal ocean water and negatively impacts the sea creatures that live within it. Sea urchins, for example, have difficulty forming the exoskeletons (hard outer shells) that protect them from certain predators; thereby causing them to decrease in number. This change impacts the ocean food chain. Scientists are aware of this threat and, because of it, are currently researching ways to reduce the negative effects of acid rain on the ocean environment.

Trees

Trees, often entire forests, are negatively affected by acid rain and the process of correction can take decades to complete. Problems occur when the rain contaminates soil and depletes essential tree growth nutrients such as calcium and magnesium. Additionally, the acid rain promotes the release of aluminum into the earth, which makes it difficult for trees to absorb water.

Trees with the highest risk for damage are those with the most exposure to the acid rain. For example, a tree on a mountain top is much more likely to be damaged than a tree located in the middle of a dense forest. However, regardless of location, large amounts of acid rain have a negative impact that can impact thousands of trees at the same time.

Structures and objects

Structures include statues, monuments, walls, and buildings. From an environmentalist perspective, structural damage is probably the least concern of acid rain because that damage usually comes in the form of lost beauty and decreased monetary value. However, this damage can lead to other problems because local residents and businesses tend to start taking less interest in the care and upkeep of their property.

It must be noted that structural damage resulting from acid rain does have a limited impact on the environment. Contaminants from affected structures, such as paint and metals, can leach into the land below; thereby creating soil pollution issues. As discussed in the first section of this book, soil pollution poses a threat to people and the environment.

Solutions

Acid rain is an environmental concern that is not clearly understood by many people. They know it is probably not good, but they are not completely sure why it has a negative impact on the environment. A good grasp of chemistry is needed to completely understand the destruction that acid rain can bring about, but all that really needs to be understood is it affects the balance of nature on land and in water. If not controlled, it could have a lasting impact on the entire ecosystem.

It is not practical to completely eliminate acid rain, but its negative impact can be mitigated by applying some corrective actions.   There are also ways to prevent it from happening; thereby negating the need for those actions. Below are some examples of corrective actions and preventative measures that are currently being used to combat acid rain.

Corrective actions

As the name implies, acid rain is acidic. When it lands on the environment it acidifies that environment. However, acidification can be neutralized with the addition of alkaline chemicals such as calcium carbonite. This chemical can be added to the ground to prevent the acidification process from taking place.

The addition of alkaline chemicals to soil usually requires human intervention, but sometimes this process is not human-induced. Natural neutralization is the reason why some earth does not experience the negative effects of acid rain. Soil rich in limestone, for example, does not acidify due to the alkalinity of that limestone. So, should lime be added to all soil that faces the potential for acid rain? The answer is no because excess amounts restrict the availability of nutrients necessary for plant growth. In short, the plants will end up being undersized and non-productive.

Another type of corrective action involves time and effort. This solution is a combination of corrective action and preventative measures because it involves waiting for the environment to change while pollution control measures are put in place to prevent further contamination. As the air becomes cleaner, the rain becomes less acidic, and the ground responds by gradually returning to its normal state. Many people do not want to hear about this type of corrective action because it essentially means doing nothing that will have an immediate impact. However, one way to counteract the negative effect of acid rain is to implement a pollution reduction plan and wait it out.

Preventative measures

The most obvious preventative measure is to reduce the amount of polluting gases and particles, specifically sulfur and nitrogen, released into the air so they are not absorbed by the rain. This can be done using cleaner fuels or less of the polluting fuels. Some sacrifices might need to be made, but those sacrifices are likely minimal when compared to the value of preserving the environment.

Another type of preventative measure involves using other sources of energy that do not release the pollutants that cause acid rain. For example, wind or solar energy can be used to generate needed electricity. If these two options are not viable, then a potential alternative is nuclear energy. The point here is that pollutants can be controlled while still generating the power necessary to run businesses, drive vehicles, or operate farms.

Summary

Acid rain is acidified rain caused by humans polluting the air. It does not pose a threat to human health, but it does have a negative acidifying effect on different aspects of the environment including water, trees, structures, and objects. This acidification process can be reversed with the use of alkaline chemicals, and it can be prevented by limiting or changing the types of fuels that pollute the air. Contrary to what some people might believe, acid rain is real and it is a threat to the natural world.

Authors' perspective

We believe that acid rain is the least environmental concern discussed in this book. We understand that it is a threat to the natural world, but it has minimal negative impact when compared to other types of pollution and it has no detrimental effects on human health. Some people would argue that something that does not negatively impact human health is not a threat, but their argument is not the reason for our position. We think acid rain is the least threatening because it is advantageous in certain ways. For example, it has sulfur compounds that suppress the production of methane. Methane is necessary for methane gas which, along with carbon dioxide, are the major greenhouse gases that produce global warming.   This impediment is due to a somewhat complex chemical reaction, but essentially the methane-emitting microbes cannot compete in the environment created by acid rain and are consequently unable to produce gas.

Another advantage of acid rain is its ability to help forests prosper. When combined with modest forest temperature increases, it has been found to make trees and other foliage more productive. Essentially, the trees have more capacity for carbon storage when the soil contains higher levels of nitrogen compounds received from the acid rain. Higher carbon storage allows the trees and surrounding foliage to experience healthy growth.

Now that we have expressed our thoughts about acid rain, we want to close by clarifying our position so readers do not think we are contradicting ourselves. We realize acid rain is a concern which is why it is discussed in this book.

However, we also believe it is not in the same category as the other threats discussed due to its potential for helping the environment.

Deforestation

Background

Deforestation occurs when forests or groups of trees are removed for the `purpose of converting the land to some type of non-forest use. The most well-known type of deforestation occurs in rainforests of tropical areas. Areas cleared are typically used for mining, logging, overpopulation (housing), or industrial developmental purposes, and the resulting effects are devastating for much of the wildlife that made these areas their home. Some people estimate that the Amazon rainforest loses about 20 square miles per year due to deforestation. This issue is at the top of many environmentalists' lists of concerns, and it has also become a popular topic of discussion in the mainstream public.

Many scientists agree that deforestation accelerates the process of global warming. Global warming occurs when the overall temperature of the earth's atmosphere increases over time. It results when increased levels of carbon dioxide and other pollutants change atmospheric conditions, also known as the greenhouse effect. Forests absorb carbon dioxide from the air, and when those forests are depleted, the carbon dioxide remains; thereby contributing to the destructive climate change alluded to by environmentalists and a substantial portion of the scientific community.

As populations increase, so does deforestation. In one way, this clearing of the land makes sense because it allows people more space to live and work. However, deforestation activities also have major consequences for the environment because natural resources are depleted and the negative impact is difficult to reverse. Without some type of intervention, deforestation is capable of destroying the natural world with little or no hope of recovery.

Effects

As noted above, deforestation promotes global warming. This warming is an environmental concern because it affects many species of animals and plants. Some of these plants and animals find it difficult to adjust to the change; thereby questioning their existence in the future if the warming continues. If they start to disappear from the earth, then the entire ecosystem could be affected...and it is difficult to predict what could then happen.

An example of the effects of global warming involves polar bears. These animals have a diet that often relies on the meat from seals that they get from the ocean. They catch these seals by patiently waiting at breathing holes in ice until the seals come up for air. Once above the water, the bears pounce on the seals and pull them onto the ice where they are consumed. Global warming is reducing the amount of ice that the bears have available, and this reduction provides seals access to other areas for breathing. If the opportunity to catch seals does not arise, then the bears are threatened with starving to death.

Another example of the impact of global warning involves pollination. Pollination takes place when pollen grains from male flowers are transferred to female flowers; thereby enabling fertilization and the production of seeds for offspring. Many flowers rely on bees to cross-pollinate so they can reproduce. Nature has made it so the bees come out of hibernation at the same time the flowers' pollinators are emerging. However, global warming has caused the bees to come out of hibernation earlier, before the flowers' pollinators have emerged; thereby preventing the cross-pollination and fertilization necessary to assure reproduction.

Deforestation also destroys animal habitats. When sections of forest are cleared, the animals have no other choice but to relocate. They end up in smaller and smaller sections of the remaining forest, and competition for food becomes intense. This competition is so fierce that some animals are forced to forage elsewhere, so they learn to lose their fear of humans and move into cities and villages in search of food. At this point, the animals become a nuisance and need to be captured and relocated or, in more severe cases, killed.

The last effect of deforestation is economic, rather than environmental, but it is still important because it affects people and businesses. Deforestation often occurs from logging and, unfortunately, much of that logging is not legal. Illegal activities include harvesting from protected areas, exceeding quotas, and logging without authorization from the proper authorities. Illegal logging has a staggering economic impact because lumber reaches markets, including the United States, without being subject to the duties and taxes heaped on companies that conduct business legally. This costs governments dearly because they do not receive the tax and duty revenue. It also costs the timber industry billions of dollars, and it threatens to put some companies out of business because they cannot compete.

Solutions

Unfortunately, regardless of what many people would like to see happen, deforestation is unlikely to go away...now or in the future. The painting of this bleak picture is based on the fact that the world is continually growing, and space is needed for that growth. Add to this the fact that clearing forests allows for the harvesting of valuable natural materials, and it is a no-brainer for those who lack concern about destroying the environment.

Deforestation might never be totally gone, but there are a few ways to reverse some of the damage. There are also ways to stop the damage from becoming so severe that corrective actions are required. Below are some examples of corrective actions and preventative measures that are currently being used to fight deforestation.

Corrective actions

The best type of corrective action is to plant one or two trees for every tree that has been removed. However, this task is easier said than done for three different reasons. First, this process is time-consuming and deforesters know that time is money, so they would rather spend that time cutting down more trees than planting new ones. Second, even if the trees do get planted, it takes decades for them to grow to the levels at which they were harvested. Third, many areas that are deforested are not intended to ever go back to their original states, so planting replacement trees is not an option.

Fortunately, some people believe strongly in reversing the negative effects of deforestation. These individuals often belong to organizations that make it their sole purpose to reduce the footprint made by man on the environment. They will go to areas where deforestation takes place and, if possible, plant trees. If not possible, they will plant trees in other areas to make up for the ones that were lost. Either way, a replacement process takes place; thereby preventing the total number of trees from diminishing.

Preventative measures

Without a doubt, the best solution for the prevention of deforestation is to stop it from happening. This can be done if deforesters have the right incentive to stop their harvesting…and that incentive is money. If money is offered to keep the forests intact, then the forests will be left alone. This is similar to the controlled farming programs that prevent the overgrazing of land by livestock and overplanting of crops by farmers. Forests remain intact and companies do not suffer the economic hardship that occurs when they are not allowed to conduct the business necessary to bring in revenue.

Another preventative measure involves corporate ethics. Companies involved in deforesting can self-monitor their actions by putting rules in place that place conservation at the forefront of their efforts. They can make it mandatory to replant trees as they remove them, make certain parts of the forest "no harvest" zones, or refrain from clearing the forests if pre-harvesting analysis shows that removing the trees will have a detrimental effect on global warming. Regardless of the type of action taken, self-imposed ethical standards have great potential for preventing deforestation.

Other preventative measures start with communication. Local people and companies involved with deforestation projects need to talk about what is needed on both sides. Greenpeace, for example, meets with local people, local governments, and forest product companies to bring about responsible foresting policies and procedures. When leaders of these companies understand the local needs, they are much more likely to take steps to reduce the destruction of the forests they are hired to harvest.

Last, but certainly not least, zero tolerance is a preventative measure that has gained a substantial following. Essentially, it means companies purchasing wood, palm oil, paper and other products produced by deforesting operations hold their suppliers accountable for their actions. These suppliers must prove that they are making sure that their efforts have minimal impact on forests and the climate. For example,

McDonald's could require their paper suppliers to measure their carbon footprint and take effective action to reduce that footprint in future operations. If this is too difficult to achieve, then there could be clean-up requirements imposed to minimize the destruction of land typically results from deforestation.

Many of the preventative measures mentioned here require political change in addition to change from people and companies. This means governments need to crack down on illegal logging and other corrupt activities related to deforestation. In short, they need to enforce the conservation rules that are in effect to move forward with the preservation agenda. Unfortunately, some governments are unable or unwilling to make the commitment necessary to change so the destruction of forests continues.

Summary

Deforestation is the process of removing trees to clear the way for mining, logging, overpopulation, or industrial developmental purposes. Entire forests are destroyed in this process and the impact is profound. Animal and plant habitats are immediately destroyed and the after-effects are even more severe due to the global warning that transpires.

Deforestation will likely never stop completely, but it can be controlled and, to a lesser extent, prevented. Replanting trees is the best way to correct the damage that has already been done, but the positive results often take decades to see. Not surprisingly, money plays a role in prevention as do politics, zero-tolerance policies, and good old-fashioned soul-searching that leads to ethical choices. If enough people, companies, and governments communicate with each other and work together, then a solution for ending the deforestation problem that currently engulfs the world is possible. However, regardless of the effort put forth so far, deforestation and its negative effects are far from over.

Authors' perspective

We believe that deforestation is at the top of the list of the environmental concerns discussed in this book. This might seem like a rather bold statement considering the impact that some of these concerns have had on the environment, but we stand by it because deforestation is in a category of its own in terms of damage that is irreversible.

When forests, especially rainforests, are cleared for non-forestry projects, they create a world of disarray for the plants and animals within them. Habitats are completely destroyed and life needs to adjust to new situations or cease to exist. However, this "readjust or perish" situation is not the major reason we feel the way we do. The crux of our belief stems from the fact that forests take centuries to rebuild…that is if they have the opportunity to rebuild. During that long period of time, generations of plants and animals are born and die, pollution impacts the environment, and people change the world to meet their own wants and needs. In combination, these changes create a situation where it is virtually impossible for a forest to restore itself to its once natural state; thereby making the negative effects of deforestation permanent while altering the ecosystem as we know it.

Water pollution

Background

Water covers almost three-fourths of the earth's surface. It is abundant, ubiquitous, and plentiful, and it is obtainable by most people in the world. However, the obtainable water is not always clean and is considered contaminated. This contamination is usually from an unnatural source, and that unnatural source is typically a result of human activities. Not surprisingly, humans are the biggest cause of water pollution.

Excluding rain and condensation, water is essentially made up of two types known as surface water and groundwater. Surface water, such as that found in lakes, streams, rivers, and oceans, is found above ground. Groundwater, such as the water used by plants and trees as a source of nutrition, is found underground.   To get a better understanding of these two types of water, they are discussed below.

Surface

Surface water consists of oceans, lakes, streams, rivers, ponds, and other above groundwater. It can be freshwater, brackish water, or saltwater, and it covers almost seventy-five percent of the earth's exterior. It contains living plant and/or animal species, and it usually supports the life around it.   For example, fish and other aquatic creatures live in it while plants, animals, and humans live around it. In fact, surface water accounts for over half of the water used by Americans in their homes and businesses.

Ground

Groundwater is the water that exists underneath the surface of the earth. It cannot be seen without going underground, but it plays an important role in the lives of plants, animals, and humans. Plants absorb it through their roots, animals drink it by digging underground, and humans extract it from wells for a variety of different reasons. However, regardless of the harvesting method, groundwater is critical for the existence of every living thing.

Surface water and groundwater make up the water that covers and resides within the earth. However, regardless of where it is located, polluted water is dangerous people to the natural environment which is why it is a major form of concern for environmentalists.

Water pollution is often identified as point-source, nonpoint-source, and transboundary. All three types are discussed below for a better understanding of their nature.

Point-source

Pollutant sources are identified as point-source when a single source can be pinpointed for causing the contamination. An example is a meat plant that discharges waste into a small lake. The wastewater has high levels of Biochemical Oxygen Demand (BOD) that are contaminating the lake; thereby depleting the oxygen available for plants and animals living in or by it. Since no other contaminants are discharged into the lake, the meat plant is the single source of pollution.

Nonpoint-source

Pollutant sources are identified as nonpoint-source when a single source cannot be pinpointed for causing the contamination. In other words, multiple polluters are discharging contaminants into the water. An example is a lake that is surrounded by two farms, three manufacturing companies, and a construction site. First, the manufacturing companies discharge chemicals into the lake. Second, sediment from the construction site drains into the lake. Last, but certainly not least, rain drainage from the farms into the lakes contains fertilizers, pesticides, and livestock waste. In short, the pollutants come from multiple sources and their combined effect is referred to as a non-point source.

Transboundary

This type of pollution is identified as being caused by short-term disasters, such as oil spills, or longtime buildup, such as slow industrial discharge that makes it into water over time. Transboundary pollution can occur when contaminated water flows between multiple states, provinces, or countries. For example, pollution that flows down a river can affect multiple areas. It might seem easy to blame the source of contamination found furthest up the river, but it is not always that simple. In many cases more pollutants are added downstream; thereby making it difficult to pinpoint one or even multiple sources as the problem.

Interestingly, contaminants can be eliminated from any of the above types of pollution using pretreatment. Pretreatment uses specific methodology to clean the source and rid it of its pollutants before it enters the water. For example, management at the meat plant mentioned as the point-source example could install a grease-trap that catches much of the physical matter before the waste exits; thereby limiting the BOD to the material that exits the trap. They could also pump oxygen into the waste that exits the trap to further reduce the BODs before it reaches the lake.

Unfortunately, many operations do not implement pretreatment procedures that are effective enough to prevent water from being polluted. This is because pretreatment is complex and expensive. It requires installation, monitoring, preventative maintenance, and repair. Management of some companies believe the risk of a fine outweighs the time and money spent on pretreatment, so they choose to do little or nothing to prevent waste from entering the water supply.

Fortunately, or unfortunately for the companies who are doing the polluting, many local and/or state governments have discharge limitations in place to prevent pollutants from discharging into the water supply. These limits are enforced via testing of the companies' wastewater as it enters sewer systems. This enforcement acts as a pollution deterrent because penalties for exceedances are imposed on the offending companies and the public images of those companies are at risk of exposure for being unethical or uncaring.

Effects

Since all living things need water to survive, water pollution is a serious concern for environmentalists. It negatively impacts plants and animals while putting humans at risk for diseases that are sometimes deadly. In fact, millions of people are slickened or killed by contaminated water every year. Many of these illnesses and deaths go virtually unnoticed because they happen in impoverished areas of the world where disease and death are common, and clean drinking water is far from the norm.

In the United States, sickness and disease from contaminated water occur more frequently than many people realize. For example, Legionnaires' disease hospitalizes thousands of Americans every year.   Essentially, this disease results from contaminated aerosols in water systems such as cooling towers and drinking fountains. The responsible bacteria for this problem are known as Legionella pneumophila, and they proliferate in warm water. These bacteria might not originate in contaminated lakes, streams, rivers, or oceans, but they contaminate closed piping systems and the end result is still polluted water.

Without a doubt, polluted water is alarming because it has many negative effects. Some of the major effects, as they pertain to plants, animals, and humans, are discussed below.

Plant and animals

Most water pollution, except for spills, begins on land. Fertilizers, pesticides, chemicals, heavy metals, and animal waste originate in farms, factories, construction sites, and urban development areas and are subsequently leaked into water via erosion, sewers, drains, and rain wash. Once in the water, they are capable of traveling long distances while destroying life along the way.

When water is polluted, plants and animals suffer. Many times this suffering works its way up the food chain from small prey to large predators. This process is known as food chain disruption, and it can lead to the death and destruction of entire species. For example, heavy metal contaminants on the bottom of a lake are eaten by tiny animals. Those metals remain in their systems until they are eaten by other animals. These predatory animals retain the metal contaminants until they are eaten by larger predators, and the transfer of metal again occurs. This cycle continues until the entire food chain is disrupted. Over time, animals at all ends of the chain have difficulty reproducing and their lives are shorted due to the heavy metals in their systems.

Food chain disruption typically occurs under the surface of the water, so it is not witnessed by people. However, people can easily see that polluted water is responsible for destroying habitats because those habitats change or disappear completely. The effects of an oil spill, for example, are obvious and it is clear the plants and animals are forced to leave the impacted area or die there. Animals are sometimes able to leave, but, unfortunately, plants are not afforded the same opportunity.

Water pollution also promotes algae growth in lakes and ponds. This growth depletes oxygen and nutrients; thereby suffocating plants and animals that share the environment. Worse yet, harmful algae growth can produce neurotoxins that impact other existing life. Turtles, for example, have been known to perish due to these toxins.

Debris is another form of pollution that affects aquatic life. Most of this debris is garbage in the form of plastic. Bags, bottles, straws, containers, caps, and lids all end up in water, especially oceans, because they are not properly disposed of or recycled. Since plastic is not biodegradable, it pollutes water, traps and suffocates marine animals, and gets eaten by fish. It does not take an environmental scientist to realize that the impact plastic has on water ecosystems is not good.

Water that is polluted by burning fossil fuel presents a huge threat to various types of shellfish. These sea creatures absorb the carbon created by the fuel; thereby making it harder for them to build the shells necessary for protection from predators. This lack of protection creates an imbalance in nature's food chain and the ecosystem is forced to change.

Humans

The residents of Flint, Michigan know well what polluted water can do to people. In 2014, due to the insufficient use of corrosion inhibitors, lead leached from the lead water pipes into the water that 100,000 residents were using for drinking and bathing. People became ill from the heavy metal in their systems, with children bearing the brunt of the problem, and it was suggested that twelve people died from Legionnaires Disease linked to the problem. It took three years and a lot of unnecessary stress to restore water to safe levels, and the problem will never be forgotten.

Lead poisoning is just one of many problems associated with water pollution. Other pollutants, both physical and chemical, find their way into water all over the world and result in health issues affecting mental health, hormone production, stomach and intestinal illnesses, and several different types of cancer. For example, mercury is a neurotoxin that can harm the brains and nervous systems of people. It gets into wastewater from businesses such as industrial sites, mining operations, and dental practices, and it can impact language and motor skills. It finds its way into humans when they eat fish containing methyl mercury, a toxic that is created from a conversion process after mercury enters water where the fish live.

Microorganisms present in polluted water that have been found to negatively impact human health include:

- *Pseudomonas pseudomallei* - causes internal pain bones and joints
- *Cryptosporidium parvum* - causes parasitic diseases in intestinal tracts
- *Giardia lamblia* - causes diarrhea and abdominal pain
- *Salmonella* - causes nausea and vomiting

Groundwater is also at risk of being polluted by farms, landfills, sanitation systems, and industrial sites. For example, harmful toxins from landfills can leach out and penetrate the soil below until they reach groundwater. This water can then seep into wells, rivers, and steams and be consumed by humans. Diseases such as typhoid and cholera can end up making people sick. Typhoid causes people to experience fever from a bacteria known as Salmonella Typhi. This fever leads to headaches, stomach aches, fatigue, and loss of appetite. If not properly treated, typhoid is fatal.

The worst part about groundwater pollution is the difficulty of correcting the problem. Eliminating the contaminants is difficult, if not impossible, to do. The pollution can remain for many years; thereby giving it more time and opportunity to seep into other sources of water such as wells, lakes, streams, and oceans. In addition to getting ill from drinking the polluted water, people who swim in it can contract rashes, pinkeye, and respiratory infections due to the contaminants coming in contact with their bodies.

In short, people use water for personal, professional, recreational, nutritional, and entertainment purposes. They might not all be using water for the same purpose, but they all have one thing in common...they want their water to be water clean.

Solutions

Fortunately, there are effective methods for correcting water pollution and preventing it from reoccurring.

Corrective actions

Surface water pollution can usually be cleaned up, but the time and money required to do this often create challenges that are difficult to overcome. Oil spills, for example, can be cleaned using oil dispersants that have the same effect as household dishwashing detergent. Surfactant molecules within the dispersants have hydrophilic (water-loving) heads that attract water and hydrophobic (water-hating) tails that repel water and attach to oil. These opposing forces break up the oil into droplets suspended in water. The hope is that these droplets will then naturally biodegrade, but, unfortunately, this is not always the case. Some oil droplets make it to the water's floor and are consumed by bottom-dwelling aquatic creatures. Once these creatures are eaten, the food chain begins the contamination cycle discussed earlier.

Other corrective action for oil spills includes:

- Lighting the oil on fire so the pollution burns off. This method works fairly well for new spills, but it becomes increasingly less effective as the oil ages. Additionally, all oil burned off results in air pollution.
- Containing the spill with a boom while skimming the oil off the top of the surface. This process is effective, but it is difficult to use for large spills. Quite simply, the money and time spent containing large areas of water can be overwhelming.

- The most interesting corrective action involves doing nothing at all. Oil is natural, and many scientists believe it will eventually break down and go back into the earth. This might be true, but issues that occur while the oil is breaking down can be catastrophic for plants and animals.

Surface water debris (plastic, wood, and other floating trash) can be physically collected and discarded. However, this takes a lot of valuable resources; thereby making the process challenging. However, the good news about physical collection is that it does work.

As noted earlier, groundwater can be difficult if not impossible to clean after it has been polluted. Sometimes the water is pumped out of the ground, cleaned, and put back into the ground. Other solutions involve adding chemicals or microorganisms to the water to destroy or neutralize the contaminants. However, in addition to the cost, these corrective actions have been less than effective in many instances, so they are often frowned upon as solutions. Unfortunately, this means the water will have to naturally clean itself as it drains into the surrounding landscape. This process could take up to a century, and a lot of environmental damage can be done during that time

Preventative measures

The world is growing at a rapid pace. This is good because growth shows that we are progressing as a society and it provides people with the resources necessary to live safe, happy, and productive lives. However, as with any type of growth, there are also growing pains. One of these pains comes in the form of pollution...and water pollution is at the top of the list.

Water pollution must be combated on a routine basis, and the best way to do this is with the use of preventative measures. These measures typically come in the form of policies, procedures, and regulatory requirements that must be implemented, monitored, and enforced if they are expected to work properly. While not 100 percent effective, they have experienced a high rate of success in many instances.

Below are some of the most effective measures for preventing water pollution.

Education – Education is a key to effective water pollution prevention because it leads to public awareness, ethical business practices, and government understanding of what people want and what can be done. Education can come in the form of face-to-face meetings, focus groups, outreach programs, webinars, or online forums. The medium is irrelevant as long as the message is communicated. An example is an outreach program conducted by a wastewater association to educate local businesses on ways to reduce their wastewater surcharges.

Government intervention – Governments are often the most effective preventative measures because they impose penalties on violators when water pollution limits are exceeded. In short, they hold violators accountable for their actions. For example, water department officials in a city issue a $2000 fine and publish the name of a metal fabrication facility for exceeding mercury limits in their wastewater discharge.

Community involvement – Community groups and organizations can be established to organize anti-water pollution programs. For example, a neighborhood gets together to plant trees (to prevent soil erosion into water), pick-up trash (to avoid trash from contaminated water), encourage recycling (to avoid recyclable material from contaminated water), and reduce chemical usage such as detergent and bleach (to avoid chemicals from going down the drain and into the sewer system).

Reduce, eliminate, or replace – Although reduction, elimination, and replacement practices apply to several different industries, these preventative measures are mostly geared toward farms. Farmers can reduce, eliminate, or replace pesticides and herbicides to limit the seepage of these chemicals into groundwater. When done properly, these measures help farmers move toward organic practices.

All of the above preventative measures require action and planning for the future. The old saying, "those who fail to plan, plan to fail," has great application in the world of water pollution prevention.

Summary

Water pollution is an abundant resource that is found all over the world, but, unfortunately, it is not always clean due to the behavior of humans. It is essentially made up of surface water, found above the earth's surface, and groundwater found below the earth's surface. However, regardless of the type, water becomes polluted when contamination enters it. This contamination can be point-source (derived from a single source), nonpoint-source (derived from multiple sources), or transboundary (derived from one or multiple sources that flow from one area to another), but, regardless of the type, plants, animals, and humans are affected. Humans face health issues from toxic bacteria, viruses, and heavy metals; plants die from oxygen depletion; and animals are forced to leave their existing habitats or perish. There are corrective actions and preventative measures that can be put in place to prevent, reduce, or eliminate water pollution, and they are becoming more and more necessary for protecting the environment as the world's population grows.

Authors' perspective

People who understand the environment and the negative impact that human activity has on it have made it clear that water pollution is a threat to the natural world. In fact, some of these people have put water pollution at the top of the list of environmental concerns. They believe that, if not addressed, contaminated water will eventually impact every person in the world.

We also view water pollution as an important environmental threat, and we agree with the above concerns. However, we think polluted water is an issue that can be dramatically improved with some changes. These changes involve the government, human communication, and education of the masses. They are not simple, but they are doable and, if managed properly, will have a lasting impact on the future of the natural world.

Our first call for change involves government action or, more specifically, government intervention. This might seem rather cliché because government involvement is everywhere, but some governments are not doing enough to reverse and prevent the water pollution problem. If rules and regulations are put into effect by governments across the glove, then companies, the major polluters of water, will change their ways of disposing waste into ground and surface water. History has shown repeatedly that "money talks," and organizations that are fined and/or temporarily shut down for their exceedances and wrongful activities will change. For example, if a company's wastewater exceeds heavy metal limits within six months, then that company is fined $5000. If they exceed the limit twice in the six months, then the fine is doubled. Obviously, 10,000 dollars is not a lot of money for some large corporations, so some of them might decide to take the fine and keep exceeding heavy metal limits. However, the government also has a rule in place that three exceedances in the same six-month period require the company to cease operations until they have a written program documenting their intended actions to rectify the problem.

The second change involves communication between businesses and communities. The sharing of information and concerns will open doors that lead to solutions for water pollution. For example, a local community could express their concern to a nearby manufacturing plant about the potential for their outdoor waste to seep into groundwater. Leaders at the plant can react by setting up methods and ways to eliminate the waste before it touches the outside ground; thereby eliminating the problem before tempers become heated and more rules and regulations are required.

The last and possibly most important change involves education. This education stems from scientists, sociologists, anthropologists, and other researchers who understand water pollution and have the ability to convey that understanding to the public, government, and businesses. When people are educated about the causes of water pollution and the damage it causes, they take a personal interest in the subject matter. This interest makes them inclined to work toward ways of reducing the impact of the problem and preventing it from growing. In terms of water pollution, knowledge is power....and that power is beneficial to people and the environment that they live within.

Regardless of the methodology used, the reduction and prevention of water pollution require planning, implementation, monitoring, and corrective action when something is not working as intended. However, if the proper procedures are in place, then we believe water pollution can be reduced to a level where plants, humans, and animals are minimally affected. It will take time and effort, but it is possible.

Air pollution

Background

Air pollution results when the atmosphere is contaminated with substances that can harm humans and the environment. These substances include gases, liquids, and solids and, not surprisingly, most are man-made. They impact the air people breathe in many ways, and that impact is virtually always negative.

In the 1970s, advertising campaigns began to push the importance of pollution by highlighting its negative effects to get people to work toward stopping it. Specific types of pollution were the focus of individual advertisements, but the one that stood out the most was air pollution. The reason air pollution stood out the most is that it affected the entire society because virtually everyone was exposed to it. People saw factory smokestacks churning out soot, car exhaust fumes spewing into the air, and tobacco smoke filling the room. The effects were real because they could be felt, smelled, and seen. After a while, air pollution was the enemy that needed to be stopped in its tracks.

Decades later, the war on air pollution is still being fought. Some major battles have been won, such as the banishing of indoor tobacco smoking, but the war still rages as more information about its negative impact is exposed.   Examples include (1) hazardous pollutants released from the air exceed those released from soil and water combined and (2) air pollution ranks as in the top ten causes of human death. These findings and others have resulted in people becoming increasingly concerned about the air they breathe. They want to do more to combat air pollution and the problems that come with it.

There are many types of air pollutants, but the major five are particulate matter, nitrogen oxides, carbon monoxide, volatile organic compounds, and sulfur oxides. Since the industrial revolution, these pollutants have done a wealth of damage to nature and, without the appropriate cleanup and preventative measures, could destroy the entire ecosystem. An example is carbon monoxide (CO) which is emitted when fuel, such as that from a diesel engine, is not completely combusted. CO is toxic to humans in terms of risk for disease, and it can even cause death.

Air pollution is often classified as primary or secondary. Primary air pollution is a direct result of a source such as industrial companies and motor vehicles. Secondary air pollution occurs when primary air pollutants (solids, liquids, or gases) are combined. Not surprisingly, the results of either type of pollution are never good and they can linger for long periods of time. An example is the smog seen in large cities. This smog is ongoing and remains in the air indefinitely based on the primary and secondary pollutants.

Air pollution often results from industrial discharge and vehicle emissions, but these are not the only causes. Agriculture is also responsible because fertilizers and pesticides emit harmful chemicals into the air that, as mentioned earlier, can also cause water pollution. Another culprit is excavation using large equipment that disrupts the soil; thereby sending physical matter, chemicals, and other contaminants into the air. The last cause worthy of mention is pollution that occurs indoors and outdoors such as that from paint, tobacco smoke, carbon monoxide, and fire.

Effects

Unfortunately, air pollution has many negative effects. In terms of human health, some effects are short-term and relatively harmless such as temporary respiratory irritation, but others are far more severe such as incurable cancer. However, the reality of air pollution is that there are no "harmless" health effects. For example, people with air pollution-related conditions that are relatively common such as asthma typically believe that those conditions are nothing less than serious.

Plants and animals also suffer from air pollution. Toxins from the air force animals to leave their natural habits in search of food and shelter, and some plants cannot proliferate. This negative effect occurs on land and water, often killing animals, plants, fish, and aquatic vegetation. Harmful alga on the water's surface, however, proliferates quite well in polluted air. It expands rapidly on lakes and ponds and destroys much of the environment in its path.

Many scientists believe that global warming has been greatly impacted by air pollution. Every day, millions of vehicles move along roads toward destinations. These vehicles release gases such as carbon dioxide into the atmosphere that trap heat and warm the earth. Industrial operations also release carbon dioxide into the air, causing the same heat-trapping effect. In short, air polluted with the carbon dioxide that results from burning fossil fuels worsens the effect of global warming.

The burning of fossil fuels also adds to the negative effects of acid rain (see the acid rain section of this book). Acid rain has a low pH that disturbs the natural balance of water, trees, and other foliage. Without this balance, the environment changes and becomes unsuitable for some plant and animal species. When rain comes in contact with polluted air, it becomes acidic and falls on the earth below...causing the destructive process to begin.

The last negative effect of air pollution worthy of mention is the ozone depletion that occurs when gasses, mostly chlorofluorocarbons and halons, pollute the air. Essentially, these gases cause chemical reactions that break down the ozone layer, rendering it incapable of peak performance. For example, chlorofluorocarbons attach to ice particles and, when those particles melt, release ozone-depleting substances. The ozone layer is important because it absorbs ultraviolet radiation which is harmful to plants, animals, and humans due to its impact on molecular structures. While ozone depletion is not part of global warming as some people erroneously believe, it is caused by the same source known as air pollution.

Solutions

Below are some major ways to correct existing air pollution and prevent it from reoccurring.

Corrective actions

Correcting air pollution once it has occurred is challenging due to the vast amount of air that needs to be treated. However, one type of corrective action that works involves the biological treatment of the contaminated air. This treatment, without going into a detailed discussion on biology or chemistry, converts the air contaminants into carbon dioxide, water, and various salt compounds. Essentially, it releases bacteria that eat contaminated substances. However, to do this, the air must be fed through a filtration device that releases the bacteria as it flows through.

As air pollution experts understand, it is difficult to pass massive amounts of air through any size or type of filter.

Preventative measures

Preventative measures work well for the reduction and elimination of air pollution. Measures that have worked in the past include the following:

- *Fees*

  Many people believe in usage fees that charge for a service based on how much of that service is used. For example, they think roads should not be paid for by the general public, but rather by fees that are charged to drivers using those roads. This same type of thinking can be applied to companies that pollute the air by charging them fees based on the amount of contaminants that they expel into the air. In short, they are being charged for their use of clean air.

- *Fines*

  Fines are similar to fees except they are typically not levied against polluters until certain thresholds are exceeded.   For example, a pH level might be limited to a maximum value of 10.0 for wastewater. Company A has wastewater with a 9.9 pH, so they are not fined. However, company B has wastewater with a pH of 10.1, so a fine of $2000 is levied against them. In most cases, pollutant limits and fines are imposed by local, state, or federal governments.

- *Alternative energy sources*

  This occurs when natural resources are used for power. These sources include wind, sun, and water, all of which do not deplete when used and can be found in most areas of the world. An example is a solar panel that converts heat from the sun into energy and stores that energy until it is needed. The best part about alternative energy sources is the fact that they do not release contaminants into the air and do not add to air pollution

- *Technology and redesign*

  This preventative measure is saved for last because it is an increasingly popular way to fight air pollution. Many companies do not want to pay fines or fees, and alternative energy is simply not enough to satisfy their power needs. To combat air pollution, they invest in technology that limits the burning of fossil fuels and the contaminants that enter the air. Examples include automobile, motorcycle, train, plane, and boat manufacturers that build more energy-efficient products and burn less fuel.

Summary

Man-made air pollution is the result of solids, liquid, or gas substances contaminating the air. It usually results from industrial discharge, vehicle emissions, agricultural activities, and excavation projects that release contaminants into the atmosphere, create chemical reactions, and alter the natural state of the air. Science has shown that air pollution negatively affects human health, plant and animal habitats, acid rain concentrations, and the ozone layer. It can be controlled and reduced, but that control requires alternative thinking, technology, and money.

Authors' perspective

We view air pollution as a major threat to the natural world, but we also see it as a problem that can be controlled with some effort. This effort will be put forth for the simple reason that everyone has to breathe air. Rich people can avoid contaminated land and, for the most part, contaminated water. They can also ignore the impact of acid rain, deforestation, and urban sprawl. However, they share the same air as everyone else, and wealth cannot change that sharing. Wealthy individuals will get involved in the fight against air pollution to protect themselves and their loved ones, and everyone will benefit.

In a sense, we view air pollution as the next cigarettes. In the mid-1950s, almost half of the adult population smoked. However, in the 1970s, the government began a war against smoking, and it has declined ever since. Public awareness decreased smoking for health reasons, and the same will be done for air pollution. As the public becomes educated, companies that pollute the air, such as chemical plants, or create products that pollute the air, such as automobile manufacturers, will be forced to bring reduce their carbon footprints or face public scrutiny and boycotts. Since any type of negative image perception has the potential to go viral on social media, these companies will change their polluting ways and the air will become cleaner.

In short, we understand the importance of air pollution and the effects it has on the natural world. Fortunately, people from all walks of life also have this understanding, and we believe that those people, in a group effort, will prevent it from destroying the environment.

Urban sprawl

Background

Urban sprawl, often consisting of suburban households and retail stores, occurs when urban areas spread into rural areas. This often seems like a sensible thing to do based on the need for space, but, unfortunately, it has many negative impacts on the environment…and some of these impacts are virtually impossible to reverse.

It should be noted that the term "urban sprawl" is thought of negatively by the general public. This negative connotation has resulted in some people opposing the use of the term and instead referring to the process as "urban growth." Urban growth puts a positive spin on the urban expansion process, but it does not protect the environment. In fact, it might even harm the environment because it allows sprawl to move forward with little resistance.

Sometimes urban sprawl is planned and can occur with limited damage to the environment. Provisions are made to preserve natural habits or incorporate them into the expansion process. However, planning is usually not the norm, especially if it requires a lot of time, inconvenience, or money.

A major cause of urban sprawl involves people's careers and is appropriately termed "job sprawl." Job sprawl occurs when people work at jobs located outside of the business districts in their cities. They want to move closer to their employers to reduce travel time, and this creates a demand for new housing. Builders happily supply this demand by building homes, and people buy those homes and move in. This influx of people creates a demand for goods and services, so businesses begin to appear in the area…and the result is flow-blown urban sprawl.

Another cause of urban sprawl is the lower cost of living. Some areas have very expensive housing and taxes, and moving outside of those areas can reduce these costs dramatically. In desirable cities, it is not uncommon for a house to cost two or three times as much as a similar house located ten miles outside of that city. In short, urban sprawl is the answer for people who do not want to give up housing quality but cannot afford to live in high-rent districts.

Interestingly, the cause of some urban sprawl has nothing to do with jobs or the cost of housing. In Detroit, for example, many people have chosen to move out of the city even though they pay higher prices for their suburban homes and drive into the city to work. This action stemmed from the deterioration of Detroit, but even as it makes a comeback some people are still more comfortable in the surrounding suburbs, and the current trend is to move even farther out. It appears that rural life is favored over city living for certain individuals.

Effects

Supporters of urban sprawl believe it creates opportunities for people who would otherwise not have those opportunities. This might be true, but the negative effects of it outweigh the positives in many instances, especially when it comes to the environment. Some of these effects, as related to humans, wildlife, and the environment, are discussed below.

Humans

As many environmentalists understand, the best way to get people to understand the negative effects something has on nature is to show how it impacts humans. Urban sprawl is a good example of this because, while it does benefit people, it also affects their health and safety which raises concerns about its value. For instance, urban sprawl means people need to do more driving to get to places, which can result in stress and road rage. This additional driving also results in less physical activity, such as walking, so obesity and hypertension are also concerns. When emergency help is needed, the right medical services are not always available because the best hospitals are often located within cities. Other negative impacts of increased driving include more accidents, fuel usage, and pollutants being emitted into the air.

A non-environmental negative effect of urban sprawl worthy of mention is its impact on communities. As people spread out and have more space, they naturally socialize less with their neighbors. Interpersonal relationships diminish and so do social norms as people become independent of one another. This is not good because trust and cooperation also tend to decrease as does social bonding. Anthropologists refer to the bonding process as social capital, and they believe it is necessary to keep communities intact.

Wildlife

Probably the biggest negative effect of urban sprawl on animals is habitat destruction. Animals lose the place where they live, and they are forced to find new areas for food, shelter from the elements, and protection from predators. The need to move on to other areas where competition for food becomes fierce. Some people believe that this results in a selection process where the strongest survive; thereby creating a new natural balance. However, this change was not the intent of nature and would not have happened without human involvement. In reality, the demands for space force the entire ecosystem to undergo man-made change.

Plants and trees also lose their habitats due to urban sprawl, but they are unable to escape their dire situations and most end up perishing unless some type of replanting program is in place. As the sprawl continues, invasive species of plants enter the area. If left uncontrolled, these invaders can take over entire areas by destroying all other species. Similar to Asian Carp taking over freshwater lakes, the results can be catastrophic for other plants that are unable to compete. Again, humans are responsible for changing the ecosystem in ways that nature never intended.

Environment

Humans, plants, and animals are all impacted by urban sprawl, but they can adapt, relocate, or be replanted in many instances. For example, trees and other greenery can be replanted to avoid a reduction in numbers, animals can move to other areas for food and shelter, and medical facilities can be built to take care of human health issues. However, land and water do not fare as well once they have been infringed upon and, unfortunately, the damage is often permanent. Soil pollution, water pollution, and air pollution take effect as people insert their dominance, and there is little or no concern about nature as it was because "progress" is occurring.

In terms of soil pollution, forests and plants are removed and replaced with more porous surfaces such as concrete and asphalt. When this happens, less rainwater is absorbed, and the natural balance of water beneath the surface is altered. Even worse, the water that is absorbed is polluted from human waste such as gas and oil; thereby affecting the quality and safety of groundwater.

Local lakes and streams are also polluted from the influx of human waste that enters the area. This contamination affects all aquatic creatures and the surrounding wildlife. Plants and animals are forced to leave the area or perish while harmful bacteria and algae proliferate. Water that was once considered clean is now off-limits for humans to swim in, and beaches are closed due to health concerns.

The increased burning of fossil fuels causes the air to become contaminated; making it unsafe for breathing in certain areas. If left untreated, smog can reach levels that impact the ozone and add to the negative effects of global warming. Interestingly, air pollution might be the most serious negative effect of urban sprawl because it cannot be seen as easily as contaminated water or soil. The "out of sight, out of mind" mentality comes into play and people simply accept what has happened without concern for restoring the natural balance of the atmosphere.

Solutions

Corrective actions

Once urban sprawl has taken place, it is difficult to correct because the damage has been done. However, it is possible to reconstruct the natural environment that has been destroyed if time and money are available. For example, areas that have been cleared can be turned into lakes or ponds, restocked with plants and animals, and allowed to obtain their natural balance over time. The same can be done for the reconstruction of forests with tree planting. Once this reconstruction is completed, these areas can be protected by law so they cannot be altered from their newly acquired natural states. Unfortunately, money trumps just about anything else in many situations, including restoration of the environment, so the road to success has some major obstacles. Add to this the fact that the time required to see these projects to completion takes decades, and it is understandable why these types of corrective actions are few and far between.

One type of corrective action that has the potential for success involves the expansion of public transportation once the urban sprawl has occurred. This does not reduce the sprawl itself, but it does help prevent the vehicle pollution that results from it. Fewer cars on the road mean less toxic emissions entering the atmosphere, and this reduces the amount of contaminated air and water.

Not surprisingly, the best way to protect the environment from urban sprawl comes from the preventative measures that are discussed next.

Preventative measures

There are a variety of methods for preventing urban sprawl and, fortunately, many of these methods are already being implemented. The key to higher interest in prevention is education because it makes people aware of the damage urban sprawl does to environments all over the world. This does not mean that society should stop expanding; it simply means that more planning needs to be in place before that expansion begins.

Urban growth boundaries, also known as smart growth, have great potential for preventing urban sprawl.   This involves local, state, or federal government setting limitations on urban expansion. For example, a city might be limited to a five-mile expansion outside of its borders. This preventative measure has been successful because it stops massive urban sprawl and requires more intense planning for protection of the environment.

Building around nature is another way to prevent the negative effects of urban sprawl. This involves incorporating nature into the expansion by preserving trees, lakes, ponds, and streams. Certain areas of land or water are protected, and provisions are set forth by the building committees to assure they remain protected after the expansion is completed. Some people consider this solution to be the best available because it allows for growth and preservation with a compromise that meets the needs of supporters and opponents of sprawl.

Expansion denial is the most effective and most controversial method for preventing the negative environmental impact of urban sprawl. In this situation, all growth is denied….with no exceptions. If there is no sprawl, then the environment cannot be impacted. However, as might be expected, there are fierce opponents to this type of preventative measure because it is very restrictive and greatly hinders the "growth of society."

The last preventative measure that warrants discussion is both interesting and unexpected. Internet shopping has reduced some of the urban sprawl that existed in the past. Shopping malls have become stagnant as people buy things online, so the additional space needed to build more of them is no longer necessary.   There was no way of predicting this change in consumer purchasing in the past, but it has become an ally of environmentalists and an unexpected asset in the fight against urban sprawl.

Summary

Urban sprawl occurs when urban areas expand into rural areas. It happens for several reasons including a need for space, job proximity, less expensive housing, and the desire to get away from the city. However, regardless of the reason, urban sprawl harms the environment. Animal habitats are destroyed during the expansion process and the resulting pollution affects human health and the existing ecosystem. There are limited options for correcting sprawl once it has occurred, but it can be controlled using planned preventative measures.

Authors' perspective

We believe that if urban sprawl is properly planned, then it can be managed and find harmony with nature. If we take the environment into account when addressing our expansion needs, then the natural world will be minimally altered. However, we also think urban sprawl is a more serious concern than many people believe it to be based on the simple basics of nature. One of our major concerns involves the wrong types of wildlife entering the newly populated areas. Animals are going to look for the easiest source of food, and human waste becomes one of the easiest. Wild animals will become less inclined to forage in the wilderness; instead choosing to feed off trash left behind by humans. Add to this the fact that some people find it "cute" to feed wild animals, and the balance of nature is altered.

People are also selective when it comes to the kinds of wild animals that look for food around their houses. For example, rabbits and deer are often accepted. However, other creatures such as raccoons, bears, coyotes, rats, and alligators are generally not as welcome. Unwelcomed animals are rounded up and relocated or destroyed.   Over time, the entire ecosystem is impacted in a way that was not intended, and the environment suffers change that is often irreversible.

We also believe that environmentalists, regardless of their efforts, will not be able to stop urban sprawl. It is going to continue because people want more space, convenience, and affordability. If they cannot get their needs met in the city, then they are going to create new suburbs...and businesses will follow. This assured growth leads us to become concerned about urban sprawl's impact on global warming. It is a known fact that populated areas of the earth add to pollution and urban sprawl is a sure way to increase the population.

Our final concern about urban sprawl stems from something other than pollution, loss of habitat, or human health concerns. In many areas, especially those that are drier due to limited rainfall, fires are a major concern, and people are often the cause of those fires. In short, our concern here is about human mistakes or carelessness. They can unintentionally start fires that destroy millions of acres of pristine environment. Many fires are started by natural occurrences such as lightning strikes, but those happenings are part of the natural balance...something that cannot be said about human mistakes or carelessness that lead to scorched countryside.

Green
Business

The Role of Sustainability

Louis Bevoc

Published by
NutriNiche System LLC

Louis Bevoc books...simple explanations of complex subjects

Note: *Green Business: The Role of Sustainability* is presented in its entirety for added discussion on the topic of environmental toxins. It was added to show how business leaders use the green concept to market and expand their organizations. It also shows that there is a trend for environmentally conscious consumers, and this trend appears to be growing in popularity.

Introduction

Green business is growing faster than it ever has in the past. It is an interesting concept because it focuses on minimizing rather than maximizing the impact of organizations. This way of thinking is perplexing to many business leaders because they are used to maximizing important areas of their organizations including income, sales, quality, and brand awareness. Their goal is to get the most "bang for their buck," and this is done by getting bigger and better.

Green business leaders are not of the "bigger and better" mentality. They strive to minimize the negative impact that their organizations have on society and the environment while becoming more transparent in their ongoing efforts for improvement. This is done by focusing on the triple-bottom-line, a term first described by John Elkington in the mid-1990s, where profits are not based solely on income and sales. The environment and society are also taken into account and these factors, along with income and sales, make up the value of businesses and determine profitability.

The concept of the triple-bottom-line needs further discussion to be fully understood...so let's move into that discussion.

Triple-bottom-line

Traditionally, the profitability (or the "bottom line") of business has been determined by profit and loss. Quite simply, expenses are subtracted from revenue and the difference is profitability. However, over the last half-century, this ideology has been challenged. Social scientists and environments believe profitability is defined by a much broader concept that takes society and the environment into account.
Based on this thinking, they implemented a process where direct and indirect costs of financial, environmental, and social impacts are combined to determine what is known as the triple-bottom-line.

An example of a business adhering to the triple-bottom-line concept is a company that invests fifty percent of all profits back into the local community. This company employs refugees from war-torn nations who are assigned the responsibility of collecting metal scrap and recycling it for cash. Society benefits from the employment found for disadvantaged refugees, the local community benefits from the donations received, the environment benefits from the recycling, and the business benefits from the profits they keep. Essentially, everyone wins in what should be a long-term endeavor.

One major challenge associated with the triple-bottom-line is that it can be difficult to accurately measure the value of social and environmental impact. Green business is based on minimizing the negative impact, and this is difficult to gauge because the maximum impact of those negatives is unknown. This means some guesswork must be involved, and guesswork is frowned upon by number-crunching people who prefer quantitative results supported by real data.

Hundreds of pages could be devoted to the concept of the triple-bottom-line, but this book is not designed for that type of detail. It focuses on green business, and green business only requires a brief understanding of the triple-bottom-line...which has now been provided.

Let's move on to the next section which focuses on sustainability as the key to the green business concept.

Sustainability

Sustainability is the thinking that everything people need is based on the natural environment, and they must find harmony with that environment to survive and thrive. One hand washes the other as humans and nature work to benefit each other. For example, people need to breathe air so they must make sure that air is kept clean for use.   If that air is too polluted, then the future of humanity is at risk.

Many of the policies related to sustainability were established by environmentalists, but over time this thinking has become part of the mainstream. The United States made sustainability a national policy in 1969 by enacting the National Environmental Policy Act. This law allows the government to oversee the environmental, social, and economic impact of human actions by implementing regulations, funding private projects, constructing public facilities, and managing the usage of land.

The branch of government responsible for establishing and enforcing rules and regulations related to sustainability is the Environmental Protection Agency (EPA). The EPA upholds this responsibility based on the following principles:

- *Protect and replenish natural resources related to water, land, air, and energy.*

- *Fund and support positive outcomes for environmental, social, and economic systems.*
- *Prevent and reduce waste, pollution, and contamination related to natural resources and the environment.*

Other nations have followed the general practices of sustainability for hundreds of years, even though most of them do not have written policies that document their commitment. These nations' actions speak louder than their words, and some of those actions came about out of sheer necessity. For example, Europeans adhered to rules of environmental conservation because they knew that they could not exist without the resources that the earth provided. Those resources were renewable, but only if a plan was in place to make sure a conservation protocol was followed. Sustainability allowed people to live off the land and it assured that future generations could do the same.

Sustainability is often a misunderstood term in business. People confuse sustainability with social responsibility because both are concerned with society and the organization benefiting from the programs that are in place. However, there is a difference between these two terms because social responsibility focuses on the present, where sustainability is more about the future. For example, a lumber yard might feel a social responsibility to purchase all wood from nations with concern for human rights. However, from a sustainability standpoint, that same lumber yard might want to prevent the world's rain forests from being over-harvesting to protect them from becoming extinct. In short, social responsibility is geared toward short-term results while sustainability is concerned with long-term outcomes.

Sustainability is the crux of this book because green business is based on it. In fact, sustainable business is often called green business because the latter term is more easily understood. People are familiar with the term "green" because the environment is at the forefront of many discussions today. Global warming is an example of a green topic that is familiar to people all over the world. The real impact of global warming is sometimes a hot topic of debate, but it cannot be ignored by companies that want to be labeled as green businesses.

There is no absolute definition of green business because all businesses are different and they are all impacted by unique variables. However, in general, businesses are considered green if they meet the following two criteria:

- *Principles of sustainability are incorporated into all major decisions.*

    This indicates the business is committed to minimizing the negative impact on people and the environment while preserving and replenishing natural resources. For example, a dental practice decides to use only mercury-free materials for tooth fillings; thereby reducing the chance that mercury will slowly seep into people's bloodstreams causing health damage. This change benefits people living today, and it offers future generations an opportunity for healthier living.

- *Products or services offered by the business replace non-green products and services offered by other businesses.*

  This indicates the business is meeting an established demand rather than a new demand; thereby minimizing the negative impact on the environment. For example, a cleaning company introduces a completely biodegradable hand soap. This product replaces hand soaps with non-biodegradable ingredients, so contaminants do not enter the sewer systems and natural sources of water are kept cleaner now and for future generations.

In the above examples, the dental firm and cleaning company attempt to positively impact the future of humans and the environment by making changes. These changes meet the needs of people today without compromising the needs of future generations. The materials used for the fillings and the hand soap are renewable, so both organizations meet the definition of a green business. Ideally, consumers are willing to pay more money for both of these products because they believe in the green concept, so the companies benefit financially.

A simple way to think about green business is the analogy of a rocket that requires three different engines to propel it into space. The first engine is made up of the people in society, the second engine is made up of the environment and the natural resources within it, and the third engine is the financial well-being of the business itself.   All three engines need to be operating simultaneously to move forward with green ideas and concepts.   When the engines run in unison, harmony is achieved and sustainability works to reduce the negative impacts on society, the environment, and the profitability of the organization. In short, a positive triple bottom line is achieved.

Green businesses create value for everyone involved. Customers, suppliers, employees, investors, and society all benefit from the positive effects...now and in the future.   The following exemplifies these benefits using an agricultural business:

  Couples & Barth is a fishery in Maine that farm raises trout for sale to supermarkets all over the region. They use environmentally friendly methods of farming that allow them to produce fish while minimizing the negative impact on people and the environment. For example, they use solar panels to produce 20 percent of the energy required to run the farm. They also use natural cleaning compounds rather than chemicals to clean the water in their ponds.

The green efforts of Couples & Barth are beneficial to people and the environment. The solar panels conserve energy and minimize the depletion of natural resources; thereby allowing those resources to be used by future generations of people. The natural cleaning compounds keep water in the ponds clean while doing minimal damage to the surrounding soil and earth. There is less pollution and soil erosion, which benefits current and future generations of people living in the surrounding area.

The fact that Couples & Barth operate as a green business allows them to charge higher prices and sell more trout than their competition. Customers are happy to support the cause because they know they are helping people and the environment. Additionally, the higher sales volume creates jobs at the farm to keep up with the product demand, and the company is financially healthy due to increased profitability.

Couples & Barth is an organization that fits the definition of a green business. They are committed to minimizing negative impact on the environment by preserving and replenishing natural resources and providing a product that meets the needs of an established market. They survive and thrive by finding true harmony with the environment, and their actions allow them to have a positive triple-bottom-line.

Couples & Barth is an example of a green business that works, but a green business in agriculture is different from those in other industries. Every green organization must tailor its processes and procedures to meet specific needs while showing concern for people and the environment. However, there are some common strategies that all organizations can use to achieve the valued green status...and those strategies are discussed in the next section.

Common strategies

Businesses need strategies to become green and maintain their green status. If these strategies are not in place, then there is nothing to separate them from other businesses that provide the same products or services.

One common misconception about green strategies is that they cost more money than they are worth. Leaders who think this way simply do not understand the green concept, and they should not attempt to make their businesses green before developing that understanding. Green strategies save money because they take advantage of the opportunities available for cost reduction. They protect businesses from violating regulatory environmental requirements, conserve resources, and save on energy-related expenses. For example, many industrial facilities pay surcharges based on the contaminants they discharge into their sewer systems. Environmentally friendly companies can replace some of the chemicals used in their facilities with natural compounds, thereby resulting in cleaner sewage discharge and lower surcharge costs. Another example is a company that turns wind into energy. Large windmills are turned by air to create power for their operations; thereby saving on energy costs that would be incurred using electricity or natural gas.

Some common strategies from green businesses are listed below. These strategies are quite simple, but they provide a framework for the implementation and maintenance of green concepts.

Establish goals

A goal is usually the end result of a strategy, but establishing that goal requires a strategy of its own. Green thinking must be behind all decision-making related to goals even though it is easy to get out of that mindset due to cost, implementation, or maintenance reasons. For example, a green manufacturing company might have a goal of paying every employee at least 40 percent more than the minimum wage established by the government. This benefits humans because workers are assured that they will earn a livable wage.

Continuous improvement

Essentially, this is the ongoing process of continually improving the products and services being offered by the organization. For green businesses, this means continually evaluating their products or services and making changes that benefit the environment of society. For example, a lawn care company that donates 50 percent of all profits to groups working to conserve natural resources might improve by requiring all lawns to be mowed with electric lawnmowers. This minimizes pollution; thereby benefitting the environment.

Teamwork

Most people who have worked in business understand that teamwork is necessary to accomplish objectives. However, green teamwork involves collaboration with the entire supply chain to benefit people or the environment. For example, a computer manufacturer that uses all recycled or refurbished components might collaborate with a distributor to produce webinars that show the benefits of green computers from an environmental standpoint.

Creativity

In many ways, creativity is similar to continuous improvement because companies use it to get better. However, green businesses must be creative to survive because they compete for a portion of a relatively small market. This creativity typically comes in the form of innovation, often using technology as the cornerstone. For example, a green pastry manufacturer might discover a new all-natural preservative that can be used to extend the shelf life of their products. In this instance, the pastry company is improving itself...but that improvement was only possible because research and development people used modern technology to make a hybrid of natural ingredients that work to preserve food.

As noted at the beginning of this section, the strategies above are simple. There is no rocket science involved with any of these methods for moving forward, but they need to be utilized if businesses want to achieve a true green status. The next section shows the importance of this status based on the influence it has on decision-making in organizations.

Paving the way

Like it or not, green concepts and ideas impact decisions made by business leaders. They are forced to take green thinking into consideration because people all over the world are concerned about society and the environment. This is not to say that companies are completely committing to going green...it simply means that if they choose to ignore people and the environment, then they risk losing a part of their customer base.

Slowly but surely, business leaders are realizing the importance of becoming environmentally friendly. They understand the upfront costs will be recouped over time via the triple-bottom-line even though they are competing with non-green organizations that do not need to meet the same requirements. Based on their actions, business leaders understand that green thinking leads to good decision-making for their organizations.

One particular aspect of green business that cannot be ignored is the fact that it stimulates a wealth of debate regarding its role, importance, and impact. There is always disagreement due to fear, uncertainty, misunderstanding, or resentment. Opponents of the green revolution see no real value in it and often do not believe the arguments for its implementation.   They regard data presented by defenders of the environment as made-up hype that is designed to scare people into jumping on the green bandwagon.   They also believe the cost of green must be passed on to the customers, and those customers simply will not pay the additional price.   However, based on consumer love for the environment, naysayer business leaders have little choice other than to become socially responsible or they risk losing a segment of their customer base.

Regardless of what business leaders believe, it is a fact that some green technology lowers costs. Examples abound in terms of energy usage. Wind and solar power are essentially free after the initial set-up costs, and this provides cost savings to the organizations that choose to utilize these energy forms. This savings shows in the triple-bottom-line, but it also shows in the traditional bottom line...a feat that some people did not think was possible when going green.

Green concepts are paving the way for a new type of thinking. Despite the challenges involved, business leaders realize the added value of green products and services. This realization is accomplished by changing mindsets. In short, business leaders view green business in a positive light by altering their perception as follows:

Customers prefer green products and services

This is likely the easiest perception to change because the facts speak for themselves. In the past, business leaders did not think customers wanted anything to do with green products or services, and they were probably right. However, times have changed and consumers are much more conscious about acting now to preserve the environment for future generations. The earth and the people who inhabit it are now at the forefront of consumer concerns, and their purchases are quite indicative of this change in thinking.

Astute business leaders have a goal of growing their organizations' sales. They watch their markets intensely and react as quickly as possible when trends develop. They see the trend of green products and services, and this has changed their perception of the green concept. "Go green" is now part of a marketing plan rather than an obscure thought.

Obstacles are seen as opportunities

This is likely the hardest perception to change because it involves a complete reversal of thinking. In general, most people think of obstacles as roadblocks that must be removed to move forward. They spend a lot of time trying to figure out how to eliminate these roadblocks and ultimately end up giving up or navigating around them to reach their destination. Either way, they lose something because giving up is failure, and navigating around something results in making sacrifices that often do not justify the achievement.

Sharp business leaders view obstacles as opportunities to improve, and that perception works well for green business. For example, a meat processing plant might have to comply with an EPA rule that requires their smokehouse to emit 25 percent less pollution within the three years. They can purchase a $20,000 air scrubber that will reduce the pollution by the required 25 percent. However, they can also purchase a $35,000 air scrubber that will reduce 60 percent of the pollution. They view the $35,000 air scrubber as an opportunity to better themselves because it will exceed EPA standards and it will also reduce the complaints from neighborhood residents who have found the smoke to be an annoyance. They purchase the more expensive scrubber even though it is tempting to adhere to the lowest environmental standards due to cost reasons.

Regulations drive the supply chain

Traditionally, leaders of companies that supply products and services to consumers have viewed regulations as a necessary cost of doing business. They conform because they are required to do so, and they absorb 100 percent of the costs in the process. However, green rules and regulations affect the entire supply chain....not just the businesses supplying the products or services.

Smart business leaders know that green regulations are not limited to their own organizations. They understand that the rules are mandatory for every company in the supply chain, from suppliers to customers, so they all need to make changes. Their mindset of making changes "because we have to" goes out the window, and their new perception is that every company is making changes to better the entire chain. It is a team effort, and every organization shares some of the responsibility; thereby lifting the sole burden off the companies that supply products and services to consumers.

Triple-bottom lines are important

Traditional bottom lines based on profitability will always be indicators of business success. Investors, stockholders, and employees view profitability as a sign of organizational health...and they make decisions to invest in or work for those organizations based on that view. This is the way it was in the past, the way it is now, and the way it will be in the future. However, green business has added a new dimension to this old thinking with the introduction of the triple-bottom-line. The triple-bottom-line takes society and the environment into account because customers are demanding more green products and services than they ever have in the past. Profitability needs to be determined based on that demand, and the traditional bottom lines do not show the entire picture.

There is little doubt that green businesses will pave the way in the future. They will continue to grow as organizations all over the world realize the importance of preserving the environment and improving human lives. A constant stream of new green ideas and concepts are being generated today, and this trend will continue as more money is spent funding green research with the expectation that the investment will be recouped over time.

Now, let's move on to the next section that suggests specific actions that businesses can take to assure the environment is better for future generations.

Reducing carbon footprints

A major goal of any green business is to decrease the damage that their products and services do to people and the environment.   One method of evaluating that damage involves measuring the amount of carbon produced by an organization. Essentially, this is done by measuring greenhouse gases (gases that keep heat from exiting the atmosphere of the earth) produced by the organization….more commonly known as measuring that organization's carbon footprint.

The term "carbon footprint" is understood by many people regardless of their experience with green business. They know the term refers to an individual or organization's impact on the environment, even though they are unsure of the exact definition. For the purposes of this book, the carbon footprint of a business is defined as:

The amount of carbon dioxide emitted by an organization that uses fossil fuels

High levels of carbon dioxide are not good for people because they can adversely affect respiratory functions in the body by displacing oxygen in the air. Based on this fact, it is rather obvious that carbon dioxide emission needs to be minimalized…and that is why this section focuses on the reduction of carbon footprints.

Fossil fuels are non-renewable sources of energy that leave a carbon footprint when burned.   Unfortunately, many different types of businesses burn large amounts of fossil fuels when they operate. Vehicles, machinery, refrigeration, and heating all require energy…and that energy typically comes from fossil fuels. That being said, the following are some ways to reduce carbon footprints in business:

Paperless communication

This involves sending electronic correspondence instead of paper. It saves money by not having to buy the paper and ink necessary for writing. More importantly, it eliminates the energy required to distribute the paper, and it saves the fossil fuels burned during the manufacturing process.

Telecommuting is a type of paperless communication that deserves mention due to its growing popularity. It is valuable for the environment because it reduces energy usage and creates a happier workforce because employees can work from just about anywhere that has internet access.

In general, paperless communication works well for reducing the carbon footprint of businesses. The minimized environmental impact and cost savings truly make it an opportunity rather than an obstacle for achieving green status.

Recycle

This refers to reusing a product rather than making it new at the expense of the environment. That expense is more complex than it might appear because it is more than just the energy needed for manufacturing. It also includes the energy needed to transport the old item to a landfill, the pollution that results during that transfer of that old item, the landfill space required to bury the old item, and the impact on the environment if the old item is not readily biodegradable. The carbon footprint expands with each step of the process, and it can be prevented with simple recycling.

Businesses need comprehensive recycling policies in place that include exploring new options because the entire world is thinking and acting greener than it ever has in the past. Consumers are demanding green products and services, and businesses need to react in a timely and efficient manner to meet those demands.

Product and process design

Product design is important because, when done properly, it eliminates waste and reduces the negative effects on the environment. For example, a rubber toy might need to have the excess rubber trimmed off after it comes out of a mold. That mold can be redesigned to minimize the waste that is trimmed. That same toy could also incorporate more environmentally friendly raw materials so it breaks down faster after it meets its final resting place in a landfill.

Processes can also be redesigned to be more environmentally friendly. Waste can be eliminated by changing the way products are made and incorporating rework back into those products. For example, a confectionary can implement a process to rework scrap candy into new batches of the same product. Additionally, the lines for packing that candy can be redesigned so fewer pieces fall on the floor and end up being disposed of in the trash.

One last aspect of product process and design that needs to be discussed involves procedures. Procedures for energy conservation need to be updated to meet the needs of green business. Lights, machines, and equipment must be turned off when they are not in use. These conservative practices are easy ways to reduce carbon footprints, but they are often ignored because employees are not in the habit of taking the appropriate action. However, they will change their habits and think about energy conservation if they are constantly reminded to do so via new procedures.

In short, businesses can reduce their carbon footprints by designing their products and processes so they utilize renewable resources and have a minimum negative impact on the environment. They need to take consumer concerns into account and make decisions with the entire product life cycle in mind. This incorporates a "recycle, rework, and reuse" mentality while thinking about energy usage, government regulations, processing, storage, and disposal. In other words, a business must consider the impact on nature from cradle-to-grave.

Avoid greenwashing

Although greenwashing is not necessarily a way to reduce carbon footprints, it needs to be mentioned because it is harmful to society and the environment. Greenwashing is a deceptive practice where organizations promote themselves as being environmentally friendly when this is not really true.

Businesses that engage in greenwashing are deceptive because they are doing more damage to the environment than they admit. An example is a company that promotes a cleaning product as all-natural when, in fact, it contains some chemicals. This type of behavior makes consumers distrust the entire green industry, and it reduces their desire to make green products and services the norm.

In short, greenwashing is fraudulent activity that is environmentally destructive and leads to people believing something that is not legitimate or true. This practice needs to be avoided, or carbon footprints will increase without any type of resistance.

Summary

Green business minimizes the negative impact of organizations on society and the environment. It makes businesses stronger by focusing on the triple-bottom-line that takes nature into account in addition to income and sales.

This book explores green business as it relates to society and the environment. It examines the triple-bottom-line, recommends common strategies for implementation and maintenance, discusses the impact on decisions of business leaders, and suggests methods for reducing carbon footprints. The text is educational and informational, and it is written for easy reader understanding at all levels.

Congratulations! You now understand more about green business....and an increasingly important concept for organizations all over the world.

Authors' perspective

We agree that green business is an increasingly important business concept worldwide. However, we also believe that it might not have as much significance as some environmentalists like to think. Yes, green business does minimize the negative impact of organizations on the environment, and this is good. However, the triple-bottom-line is far from being embraced by business leaders. Stockholders want a return on their investment, and that return still comes in the form of money...regardless of its impact on the environment.